AF449067

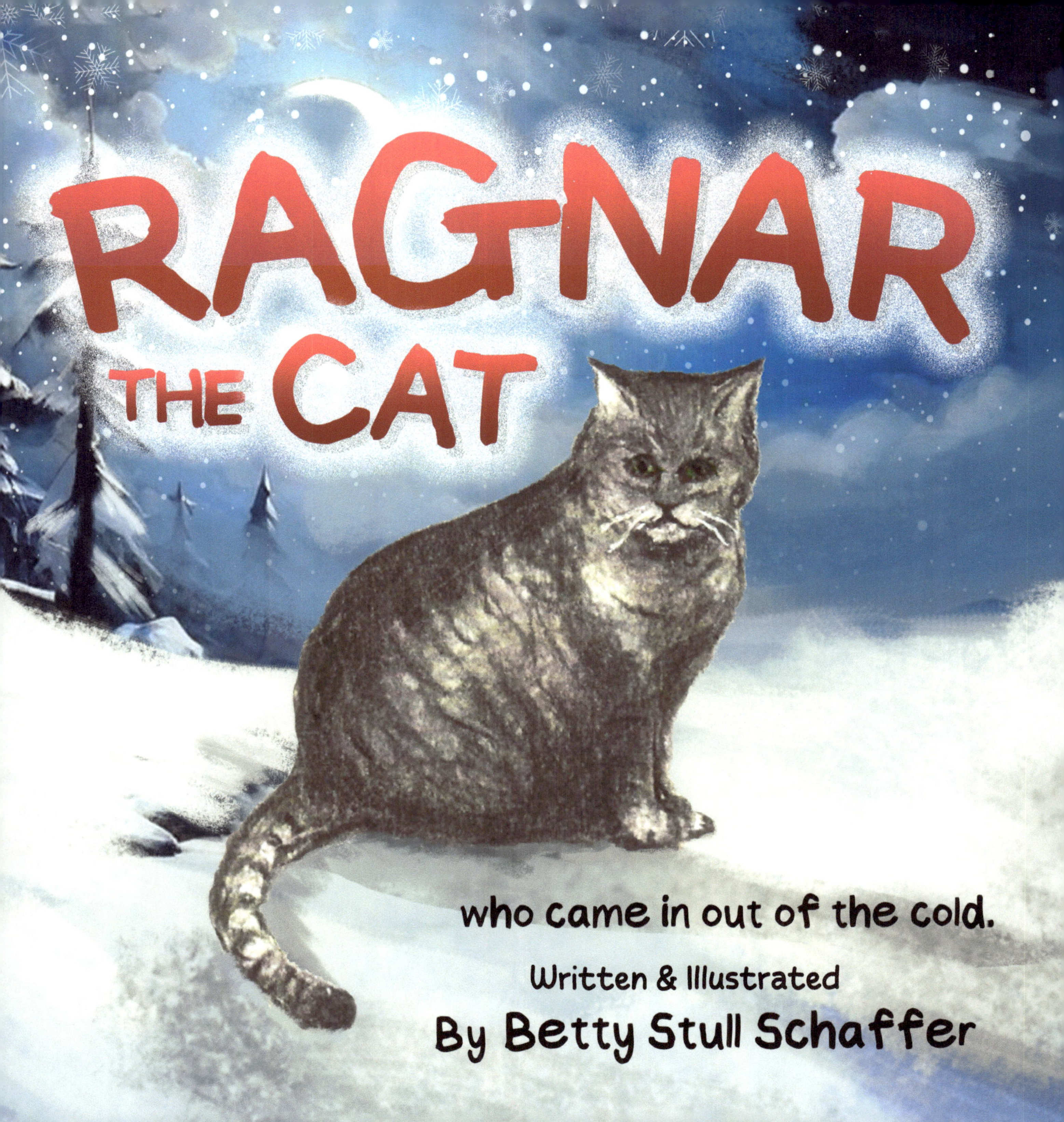

RAGNAR THE CAT

who came in out of the cold.

Written & Illustrated
By Betty Stull Schaffer

This book is dedicated to my daughter Sadie and her cat Ragnar.

Ragnar is a big gray cat who was named after a Viking King. He lives with Sadie in a little house on a very old farm. The farm is so old that the big barns that were once on it have all fallen down. There is still an apple orchard, a vegetable garden, and three black sheep.

On a very cold night in the middle of the winter, Sadie let Ragnar out for his usual evening trip outdoors. The temperature was below zero, and that is really cold.

Sadie was tired and sleepy. She put wood in the stove and went to bed. She forgot to call Ragnar in.

There are reasons, besides the cold temperature, to bring Ragnar inside for the night. There are hungry night creatures like big owls and coyotes who are looking for small animals.

When Ragnar was ready to come back into the house, the door did not open. Sadie had not called. What to do? No problem.

This is a very old house, and it has an old-fashioned thumb latch.
Ragnar knows how to open the door.

Ragnar reached up, up and up. He couldn't quite reach it, standing
on his hind feet. He needed to give a little jump, which he did.

The door swung open with Ragnar hanging on it. Ragnar dropped to the floor. He was in the nice, warm kitchen.

He sat for a moment and looked at the pantry door. The pantry is where Sadie keeps Ragnar's cat food, but he had not been able to tell her to keep it in a container that he can open.

So Ragnar went to his favorite warm spot by the wood stove in the living room and went to sleep.

Sadie woke up in the night and was cold. When she entered the kitchen, it was very, very cold. She could see why. The door to the outside was wide open. She remembered then that she had let Ragnar out but not in. She quickly closed the door.

16

She tried the pump at the sink. No water came out of it. It was frozen. Frozen water pipes can burst. That is a serious problem.

Ragnar was awake by now and came and began to wind around Sadie's legs and purr. Perhaps Sadie would open the pantry door and feed him.

Instead, she seemed worried about that hand pump at the kitchen sink. She began to pour hot water into it.

Ragnar sat and watched this strange procedure.

When Sadie began pumping water from the little pump, she knew that the pipe was no longer frozen; she looked very happy.

Then Sadie gave Ragnar something to eat.

Sadie said, "I am sorry that I did not call you in tonight, but I do wish you knew how to close the door."

The end of a true story about a real cat.

About the Author

Betty Stull Schaffer began drawing at an early age and has never stopped. While raising a family of six children she still managed to draw and paint whenever she could. Eventually, she had more time to dedicate to art which included writing and illustrating children's books. Now, well into her nineties, and with encouragement from her children and grandchildren, she is publishing one of their favorite books, "Ragnar the Cat".

She illustrated her first published children's book in 1967. The book, "Five Cent, Five Cent", written by Edna Walker Chandler had a second printing in 1972. It was published by Albert Whitman & Company and printed in USA. L.C. Catalog Card Number 67.17414, and was published simultaneously in Canada by George J. McLeod LTD, Toronto

Betty was born in Indiana, grew up in Ohio, and graduated with an art degree from Wittenberg University. As the wife of a missionary doctor she spent eleven years raising her children in Liberia, West Africa. Since the 1980's she has called southwest Massachusetts her home. Her children continue to encourage her creativity and it was her daughter's cat, Ragnar, who inspired this story.